INSIDE COLLEGE FOOTBALL

OKLAHOMA SOONERS

BY TODD RYAN

SportsZone

An Imprint of Abdo Publishing
abdobooks.com

abdobooks.com

Published by Abdo Publishing, a division of ABDO, PO Box 398166, Minneapolis, Minnesota 55439.

Printed in the United States of America, North Mankato, Minnesota
032020
092020

Cover Photo: John Williamson/AP Images
Interior Photos: J. Pat Carter/AP Images, 5, 15; Tony Gutierrez/AP Images, 7; Amy E. Conn/AP Images, 9; AP Images, 11, 18, 25, 43; Matty Zimmerman/AP Images, 17; William P. Straeter/AP Images, 20; Harold Valentine/AP Images, 23; Charles Bennett/AP Images, 27; Paul Southerland/AP Images, 30; Brian Bahr/Allsport/Getty Images Sport/Getty Images, 33; Ty Russell/The Daily Oklahoman/AP Images, 35; Ty Russell/AP Images, 36; Sue Ogrocki/AP Images, 38, 41

Editor: Patrick Donnelly
Series Designer: Nikki Nordby

Library of Congress Control Number: 2019954388

Publisher's Cataloging-in-Publication Data

Names: Ryan, Todd, author.
Title: Oklahoma Sooners / by Todd Ryan
Description: Minneapolis, Minnesota : Abdo Publishing, 2021 | Series: Inside college football | Includes online resources and index.
Identifiers: ISBN 9781532192487 (lib. bdg.) | ISBN 9781644944707 (pbk.) | ISBN 9781098210380 (ebook)
Subjects: LCSH: Oklahoma Sooners (Football team)--Juvenile literature. | Universities and colleges--Athletics--Juvenile literature. | American football--Juvenile literature. | College sports--United States--History--Juvenile literature.
Classification: DDC 796.33263--dc23

TABLE OF CONTENTS

CHAPTER 1

STOOPS STEERS SOONERS TO SUCCESS

The Oklahoma Sooners were no strangers to being at the top of the college football world. But times were tough during the 1990s in Norman, Oklahoma. The Sooners had just five winning seasons in that 10-year span. They played in only four bowl games. And they won just two.

But then Bob Stoops was hired as head coach in 1999. By the end of his second season in Norman, he had the Sooners playing for their seventh national championship. Oklahoma was set to face the second-ranked Florida State Seminoles in the Orange Bowl in Miami, Florida, on January 3, 2001.

The Seminoles were a formidable opponent. They had won the national championship the year before. And they had been ranked in the top four in the final Associated Press (AP) Poll 14 years in

Oklahoma linebacker Torrance Marshall returns an interception for a touchdown during a 2000 win against Texas A&M.

SOONERS
10

"RED OCTOBER"

After starting the 2000 season 4–0, the Sooners faced a difficult month against three teams ranked in the top 10 in the nation. But Oklahoma beat all three of them during what came to be known as "Red October." This included wins over second-ranked Kansas State and top-ranked Nebraska in consecutive weeks. It was the first time in National Collegiate Athletic Association (NCAA) history that a team had beaten the top two teams in the AP Poll two weeks in a row.

a row heading into the 2000 season. So even though Oklahoma was ranked No. 1 at the time, Florida State's fast, athletic team was favored by more than 10 points.

Stoops's experience as defensive coordinator at Florida was a big benefit for the Sooners, though. He had helped the Gators win the 1996 national championship. And he had faced the high-scoring Florida State offense several times, so he knew how to defend against it. Oklahoma fans were optimistic going into the game.

The 76,835 fans who packed Miami's Pro Player Stadium that night expected the two high-flying offenses to trade scores throughout the game. Florida State's Heisman Trophy–winning quarterback Chris Weinke got the game off to a fast start with a 35-yard completion to wide receiver Atrews Bell on the first play of the game. But the free-flowing nature of the game stopped there. Instead, it was the two elite defenses that took over.

Oklahoma senior linebacker Torrance Marshall intercepted a Weinke pass in the first quarter. The Sooners' offense was then able

× Oklahoma quarterback Josh Heupel drops back during the first quarter of the 2001 Orange Bowl against Florida State.

to get close enough for kicker Tim Duncan to make a 27-yard field goal. That turned out to be the only scoring in the first half.

After halftime, the defenses picked up where they left off. Duncan hit another field goal in the third quarter. The 42-yard kick extended Oklahoma's lead to 6–0. And it was the only score of the quarter.

STOOPS'S BOWL STREAK

Bob Stoops had tremendous success as a defensive coordinator at Florida. He brought that success with him to Oklahoma when he became coach before the 1999 season. He brought the Sooners to bowl games in all 18 seasons he coached. That included four national championship games.

The Sooners finally broke through in the final 15 minutes. All-America linebacker Rocky Calmus caused Weinke to fumble deep in Seminoles territory. Soon after, sophomore running back Quentin Griffin burst into the end zone with 8:30 to play. That put Oklahoma up 13–0.

Florida State was able to register a safety with 55 seconds left in the game. That made the score 13–2. But it was too little, too late. That became the final score as Sooners defensive back Ontei Jones intercepted Weinke with 16 seconds left to end the contest.

"Our players recognize that the history of Oklahoma is winning championships," Stoops said after the game. "We already had six. Now we have seven."

Oklahoma quarterback Josh Heupel did not put up great numbers on the night. But he had done enough to give the Sooners defense a rest. He completed 25 of 39 passes for 214 yards. More importantly, he kept the ball away from the high-powered Seminoles offense. The Sooners' offense held the ball for 13 more minutes than Florida State.

From left, coach Bob Stoops, J. T. Thatcher, and Ontei Jones celebrate after Oklahoma won the 2000 national title.

As they had all year, the Sooners won the game with their suffocating defense. Marshall made six tackles to go along with his interception. He was named the game's Most Valuable Player (MVP). Oklahoma disguised its coverages all night. The Sooners had players pretend they were going to rush the quarterback, then drop back to cover receivers. "It seemed like they had radar," Bell said after the game. "Everything we tried, they were ready for."

The win left Oklahoma as the only undefeated team in the country. In just his second year, Stoops had brought the Sooners back to the top of the college football world. He was the latest in a long line of successful coaches at Oklahoma.

CHAPTER 2

A SMALL START

The first football game in the University of Oklahoma's history was played on November 7, 1895. The opponent was a team from Oklahoma City. It was made up of local high school players and players from nearby Methodist College. But the Oklahoma City team beat up on Oklahoma 34–0.

College football, both as a sport and in its organization, looked very different in its early years. The game itself resembled rugby more than today's football. There also were no massive stadiums, prime-time television games, or major conferences. For the next four years, Oklahoma played at least two games per season. The team, then sometimes called the Rough Riders, went 8–2 in those first five years.

Vernon L. Parrington became Oklahoma's first full-time football coach in 1897. Parrington made sure the team lived up to its Rough Riders name. He ran hard practices and made the players spend a lot of time on the field.

The Oklahoma defense corrals a Tennessee ball carrier during the Orange Bowl on January 2, 1939.

67

RABID RIVALRIES

The Sooners have piled up hundreds of victories over the years. And they have managed to make a few enemies along the way. One of Oklahoma's biggest rivals is Texas. The Red River Rivalry, as it's known, is named for the river that runs along part of the Oklahoma-Texas border. Since their first meeting in 1900, the Sooners and Longhorns have become two of the most successful programs in the history of college football. In 1912 the schools moved their game to Dallas, Texas, where a larger stadium could hold more fans. They have faced off in Dallas every year since 1929.

The Sooners also have a strong rivalry with Oklahoma State. Those two meet every year in what is known as the Bedlam Series. The first Bedlam game was in 1904. Oklahoma beat Oklahoma State—which was then known as Oklahoma A&M—75–0. It remained the biggest win in the history of the series through 2019. The series has been lopsided, however, with Oklahoma holding an all-time record of 81–18–7.

Oklahoma started playing more games in 1900. Perhaps the most important one was on October 10 of that year. That is when Oklahoma played Texas for the first time. Texas won the game 28–2. The teams would go on to play each other many more times over the next 100-plus years. Many consider their annual Red River Rivalry game to be one of the best in college football.

A major turning point in school history took place in 1905 when Bennie Owen was hired to coach the Sooners. He held that position until 1926. Through 2019 no coach had led the Sooners for longer.

In his 22 seasons, Owen's teams went 122–54–16. Another important Oklahoma tradition began in 1908. That is when the school's sports teams adopted the "Sooners" nickname.

The Sooners won a lot of games under Owen. And the players leading the team started to get some national recognition. In 1913 senior fullback Claude Reeds became the first Sooner to be named an All-American. Reeds was listed as a fullback. However, he confused teams by often throwing the ball. He sometimes played end as well, and he even punted for the Sooners.

Two of Owen's best seasons came when Oklahoma joined the Southwest Conference in 1914. The team went 9–1–1 in its first year in the conference. The next year, the Sooners went 10–0. They tied with Baylor for their first conference championship. Three years later, they tied for the conference championship again, this time with Texas.

WHAT IS A SOONER?

The name "Oklahoma" comes from the Choctaw words *okla* and *homma*, which translates to "red people." In the 1800s, American Indians throughout the South and Southeast United States were forcibly removed from their land by the US government and settled in the land now known as Oklahoma. Eventually, that arrangement was overturned. In 1889 the federal government allowed white settlers to claim space in the new Oklahoma Territory. "Sooners" were people who tried to claim the land before the prescribed date. The term came to mean somebody who was energetic and a hard worker. In 1908 Oklahoma's sports teams officially adopted the Sooners nickname.

OWEN FIELD

The Sooners started playing at the site of Gaylord Family–Oklahoma Memorial Stadium before it was even finished. The team played its first game at that location in 1923. Two years later, it played in front of the stands for the first time. Initially, the stadium had only 16,000 seats. Now 80,126 people can fit inside to watch the Sooners play. Memorial Stadium is named in honor of people from the school who died serving in World War I (1914–1918). The Gaylord Family donated money to help with stadium renovations in 2002, and their name was added that year.

The Sooners spent six years in the Southwest Conference. Then, in 1920, they joined the Missouri Valley Intercollegiate Athletic Association (MVIAA). They got started on the right foot with a 6–0–1 season. That was good enough to win the conference title. Two All-Americans, halfback Phil White and tackle Roy "Soupy" Smoot, led the way.

The Sooners spent eight years in the MVIAA. Then they became one of the first members of the new Big 6 Conference. Although the league would change names as it added teams over the years, it remained the Sooners' conference as of 2019.

Owen retired as Oklahoma's football coach after the 1926 season, just before the move to the Big 6. He decided to become the school's athletic director. But his influence was felt during every single home game for years to come. That is because Owen helped organize the funding to pay for what became the school's football field complex. In 1923 the field was named Owen Field in honor of the coach.

The Oklahoma football team began playing home games at Owen Field in 1923. It still plays there today.

Even though he was still around the university, Owen's presence on the sidelines was missed. The Sooners had just 11 winning seasons over the next 20 years. Coaches Adrian Lindsey, Lewie Hardage, and Biff Jones did not have much success. But Tom Stidham briefly turned around the program when he coached from 1937 to 1940.

It was under Stidham that Oklahoma went to its first bowl game. In the Orange Bowl after the 1938 season, Tennessee shut out the Sooners 17–0. That was Oklahoma's only loss of the year. The team finished 10–1 and ranked fourth in the final AP Poll. The next year, Oklahoma finished 6–2–1, earning it the No. 19 ranking in the final AP Poll. It was the last time the Sooners would be ranked for a while.

The Sooners went through five up-and-down years under coach Snorter Luster. Then Jim Tatum stepped in and took the Sooners to their second bowl game in 1946. Oklahoma beat North Carolina State 34–13 in the Gator Bowl. That finished off an 8–3 season. But Tatum left after one year to take the head coaching job at Maryland. In came Bud Wilkinson, and everything changed.

CHAPTER 3

WILKINSON'S WINNING WAYS

Oklahoma had not been able to win consistently since Bennie Owen's move to athletic director. The team went through six head coaches in the 21 years following Owen's switch. None of them had stayed on longer than five years.

Oklahoma finally found a lasting coach in Bud Wilkinson. Wilkinson joined the Oklahoma staff in 1946 as an assistant coach under his friend Jim Tatum. He became head coach when Tatum left one year later. Over the course of his career, Wilkinson would lead the Sooners to places that no other team in college football had gone before.

It quickly became clear that the Sooners had the will. In just his second year, Wilkinson led Oklahoma to a 10–1 season. That included a 14–6 win over North Carolina in the Sugar Bowl following the 1948 season. Oklahoma went back to the Sugar Bowl

The American Football Coaches Association named Bud Wilkinson the National Coach of the Year in 1949.

World-Telegram and
NEW YORK WORLD-TELEGRAM AND THE SUN, THURSDAY, JANUARY 12,
BUD WILK
ACH OF
THE WINNER!

Oklahoma halfback Billy Vessels runs around the Colorado defense during a 1950 game.

after the 1949 and 1950 seasons as well. But it was the last of the three that was most important.

In 1949 the Sooners had finished the season undefeated. Wilkinson was named national Coach of the Year. The only problem was that Notre Dame had been undefeated, too. As such, the

Sooners ended up finishing second in the final AP Poll. There was no dedicated national championship game at the time, so Notre Dame claimed the title.

There would be no finishing second the next year for Oklahoma, though. The Sooners made it through the 1950 regular season undefeated. That included wins over three ranked teams. Oklahoma had four All-Americans on its roster that year. Fullback Leon Heath and tackle Jim Weatherall led the No. 8 scoring offense in the country. Safety Buddy Jones and end Frankie Anderson anchored a strong defense.

Oklahoma earned a chance to win its third straight Sugar Bowl. But the offense fell flat in a 13–7 loss to third-ranked Kentucky. College football can often be unpredictable, though. In the season's final AP Poll, the 10–1 Sooners were still named the national champions. And Wilkinson was just getting started.

The 1953 Sooners started the season with a loss and a tie. But a 19–14 win over Texas got them rolling. That momentum would not stop for a while. From 1953 to 1957, the Sooners won an incredible 47 straight games.

BILLY VESSELS

In 1952 senior halfback Billy "Curly" Vessels became the first Sooner to win the Heisman Trophy as the best player in college football. He rushed for 1,072 yards and 17 touchdowns, caught seven passes for 165 yards and a touchdown, and even completed seven passes—two for touchdowns—that season. Vessels's contributions helped the Sooners lead the nation in scoring at 40.7 points per game.

Oklahoma's Tommy McDonald outruns a defender during a 1954 game in Kansas. The Sooners won 65–0.

No team had matched that feat through 2019. Many consider that five-year stretch to be the most dominant in college football history.

The Sooners finished the 1953 season 9–1–1. They finished sixth in the country in scoring and allowed the fourth-fewest points per game. Oklahoma maintained its spot in the top 10 in both areas for the next three years. In 1954 Oklahoma went a perfect 10–0. But two other teams also went undefeated that season, and Oklahoma finished third in the AP Poll.

A lot of key players from the 1954 undefeated team had been seniors. Wilkinson did not expect the winning streak to continue. "I don't think we're going to be nearly as good a football team as people think," he said before the start of the 1955 season.

But he was wrong. The Sooners averaged 35 points per game on offense that season. That was more than any other team in the country. And they had the defense to match. Oklahoma's opponents scored a total of 60 points all season.

RAMPANT RUSHING

All-American halfback Tommy McDonald led the Sooners in rushing for the second straight season in 1956, when he ran for 853 yards. But he could not have done it without the help of three All-America linemen—center Jerry Tubbs and guards Ed Gray and Bill Krisher. "Our line is the best," McDonald said. "I'm proud to run behind them."

On January 2, 1956, Wilkinson led the top-ranked Sooners against third-ranked Maryland in the Orange Bowl. Both teams were undefeated, but Oklahoma justified its top ranking by winning 20–6 that night in Miami. Wilkinson had led the team to an 11–0 record and a second national championship.

The winning streak had reached 30 when Oklahoma opened the 1956 season. All-American senior halfback Tommy McDonald once again led the Sooners' offense. He had become the first Oklahoma player to score a touchdown in every game of a season in 1955. He also led the team in rushing yards and was named an All-American that year. In 1956 he repeated both of those feats.

BUD WILKINSON

Bud Wilkinson spent 17 years coaching at Oklahoma. He led the team to a 145–29–4 record, including a 6–2 record in bowl games. The Sooners won an incredible 47 games in a row from 1953 to 1957. But that was not Wilkinson's only streak. The Sooners were also undefeated in 74 conference games from 1946 to 1959 (Jim Tatum was the coach in 1946). They went 72–0–2 during that span and won 14 straight conference championships starting in 1946.

Wilkinson recruited mainly in the middle of the country. Most players came from within approximately 150 miles (241 km) of Oklahoma's campus in Norman. Even with those self-imposed limits, he was able to win the school its first three national championships in 1950, 1955, and 1956.

The Sooners' rushing attack helped them score more than 46 points per game. That led the nation for the second year in a row. And just like in 1955, the defense was outstanding, giving up only 51 total points in 10 games. The Sooners shut out six teams that season and won all but two games by at least 36 points. Oklahoma came into the season ranked first in the AP Poll. And its 10–0 record ensured that it ended the season that way, too. The Sooners were national champions for a third time.

For much of 1957, Oklahoma appeared to be on its way to another undefeated season. The Sooners won their first seven games to push the winning streak to 47. But then Notre Dame came

Oklahoma coach Bud Wilkinson crouches among his players before starting practice ahead of the 1959 Orange Bowl.

to Norman and left town with a 7–0 victory, snapping the Sooners' record run.

Still, Oklahoma went 10–1, won the Orange Bowl, and finished fourth in the nation. The Sooners had a similar season in 1958, again finishing 10–1 and winning the Orange Bowl.

But even Wilkinson went through some tough times. The Sooners went a combined 31–19 over the next five years. Many teams would be happy with that record. However, it was a step down for the Sooners, and it included two losing seasons. Wilkinson finally retired from coaching after the 1963 season. But it was not long before a new coach came and took the Sooners back to the top.

CHAPTER 4

SWITZER'S SOONERS

Bud Wilkinson had turned Oklahoma into one of the best college football programs in the country. But the Sooners had trouble keeping the tradition going in the years immediately after Wilkinson left. After three disappointing seasons, Chuck Fairbanks was named head coach in 1967. And he quickly turned the program back in the right direction.

One of the reasons for the turnaround was star running back Steve Owens. He played for Oklahoma from 1967 to 1969. In his last season, he ran for 1,523 yards and scored 23 touchdowns. That was enough to earn Owens the Heisman Trophy.

Fairbanks began to use a style of offense called the wishbone in 1970. It was a rushing attack that other teams had a lot of trouble stopping. Fairbanks's best seasons with Oklahoma were 1971 and 1972. The Sooners' offense in 1971 was one of the

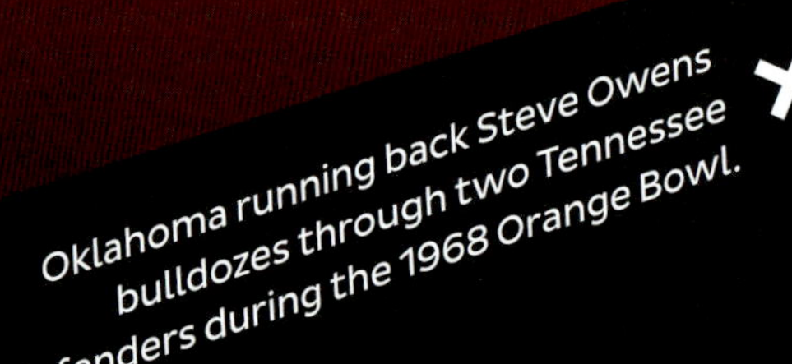

Oklahoma running back Steve Owens bulldozes through two Tennessee defenders during the 1968 Orange Bowl.

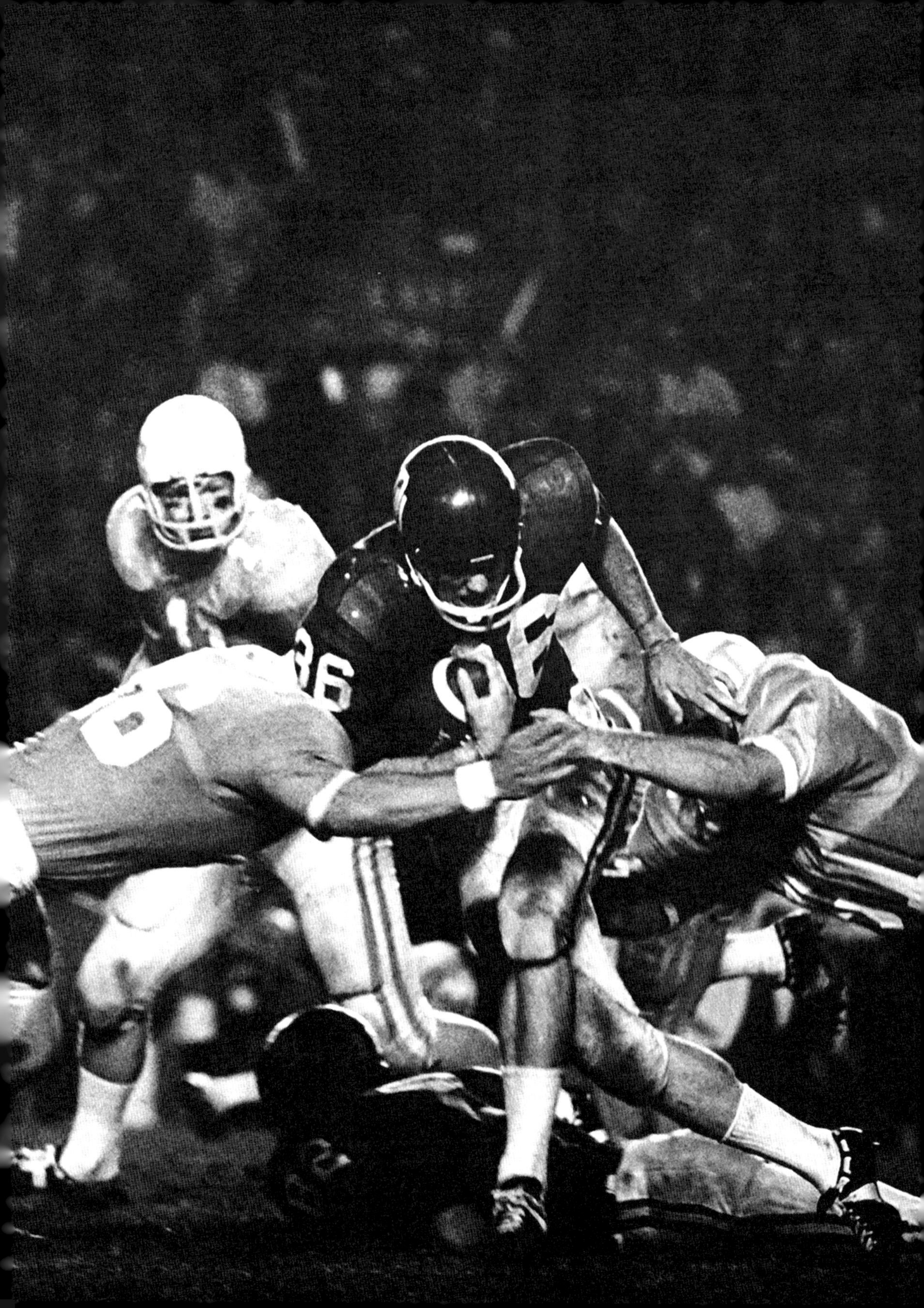

CHUCK FAIRBANKS

Bud Wilkinson and Barry Switzer might have had more long-term success at Oklahoma, but Chuck Fairbanks accomplished a lot in his six years as coach. He led the Sooners to a 52–15–1 record. That included a 34–8 conference record and a 3–1–1 mark in bowl games. Through 2019 his .772 career winning percentage remained the fourth highest in Sooners history among coaches who led the team for at least five seasons.

best college football had ever seen. The team averaged 566.5 yards per game and broke several records that season. Junior running back Greg Pruitt rushed for 1,760 yards and 18 touchdowns on just 196 attempts—an eye-popping average of 9.0 yards per carry. Quarterback Jack Mildren added 1,289 rushing yards and 20 touchdowns on the ground, plus 10 more scoring strikes through the air.

Oklahoma's biggest test was against Nebraska in what came to be known as "The Game of the Century." The teams were becoming fierce rivals after playing many important games against each other in recent years. Both were undefeated heading into the 1971 Thanksgiving Day game at Norman. Nebraska was ranked No. 1 in the nation, and Oklahoma was ranked second. The winner would go to the Orange Bowl. Nebraska scored in the final minutes of the game to steal a 35–31 victory from the Sooners. Oklahoma went on to win the Sugar Bowl, finish 11–1, and end the season ranked second in the final AP Poll behind Nebraska.

The 1972 Sooners had another great season. They again finished 11–1. Their only stumble was a 20–14 loss at ninth-ranked Colorado on October 21. But Oklahoma beat six other ranked teams that year,

Oklahoma running back Greg Pruitt rips through the Texas line en route to one of his three touchdowns in a 1971 game.

including fifth-ranked Penn State in the Sugar Bowl. The Sooners again found themselves ranked second at the end of the season.

Fairbanks had brought Oklahoma back to prominence with the wishbone offense. He was so successful that people outside college football were taking notice. In 1973 he left Oklahoma for the New England Patriots in the National Football League (NFL). But the Sooners did not miss a beat with new coach Barry Switzer.

THE WISHBONE OFFENSE

In 1968 Texas assistant Emory Bellard created the wishbone formation to take full advantage of the Longhorns' wealth of talented running backs. The wishbone formation uses three running backs. They line up in a "Y" shape—the same general shape as a wishbone in a turkey. The fullback lines up behind the quarterback. The other two backs line up behind the fullback on either side. This gives the quarterback three different players to whom he can hand off the ball. In 1970 Sooners coach Chuck Fairbanks and offensive coordinator Barry Switzer decided to use the formation at Oklahoma.

Switzer had been Oklahoma's offensive coordinator since 1967. He was one of the masterminds behind the Sooners' use of the wishbone formation. And he continued to run the offense well as head coach. In fact, Switzer's first year was almost perfect. Running backs Waymon Clark and Joe Washington carried on the rushing tradition by running for more than 1,000 yards each. Sophomore quarterback Steve Davis was also dangerous with his legs. He tallied 887 yards on the ground. The Sooners finished the 1973 season 10–0–1 and third in the AP Poll.

Nobody stopped the Sooners in 1974. They led the nation in offense with 43 points per game. They also finished fifth in the nation in scoring defense, allowing just over eight points per game. Oklahoma was ranked first in the preseason AP Poll. It ended the season that way, too. Oklahoma went a perfect 11–0 and won its fourth national title.

Switzer and the Sooners were not done winning championships. The team won its first eight games in the next season. That gave

THE SELMON BROTHERS

Brothers Lucious, Dewey, and Lee Roy Selmon helped Barry Switzer get off to an undefeated start as head coach at Oklahoma. Lucious was the oldest of the three. He was an All-America nose guard in 1973. He also won the national Defensive Player of the Year Award that year. The New England Patriots—led by former Sooners coach Chuck Fairbanks—selected him in the 1974 NFL Draft. The family's influence at Oklahoma carried on with nose guard Dewey and defensive tackle Lee Roy. Both were key to the Sooners' back-to-back championships in 1974 and 1975. Both were also All-Americans during those championship years. The two kept playing together after college was over. The Tampa Bay Buccaneers took Lee Roy first overall in the 1976 NFL Draft. They then took Dewey, who was one year older, in the second round.

Switzer a 30-game unbeaten streak to start his head-coaching career. But it came to an end when Kansas upset Oklahoma at home 23–3.

The Sooners won their next two games and earned a spot in the Orange Bowl. They were ranked third and met fifth-ranked Michigan. It was a tight, low-scoring contest. Oklahoma came away with a 14–6 win. Luckily for the Sooners, top-ranked Ohio State lost in the Rose Bowl. That led to Oklahoma once again being voted as the top team in the nation. The Sooners had not been perfect. But they had been good enough to become the first team in NCAA history to win back-to-back championships twice.

Oklahoma halfback Billy Sims rushes during a 1979 game. He won the 1978 Heisman Trophy.

The wins kept coming for Switzer and the Sooners over the next five years. The team did not drop more than two games in any of those seasons. And it finished in the top 10 of the AP Poll each year. The Sooners were 4–1 in bowl games during that span, winning the Fiesta Bowl once and the Orange Bowl three times. In 1978 junior halfback Billy Sims had one of the best seasons in Oklahoma history.

He scored 20 touchdowns and set a Big 8 Conference rushing record with 1,762 yards. Sims won the Heisman Trophy that season.

After a brief rough patch, the Sooners were back among the elite in 1985. As usual, strong rushing led the offense. Freshman quarterback Jamelle Holieway guided the wishbone attack. He threw for 517 yards and rushed for 862. Sophomore running back Lydell Carr led the team in rushing with 883 yards. The nation's second-ranked defense featured three All-Americans in linebacker Brian Bosworth, defensive end Kevin Murphy, and defensive tackle Tony Casillas.

The Sooners were the preseason No. 1 pick in the AP Poll. But they lost to the Miami Hurricanes in the fourth week of the season. That would be Oklahoma's only loss that year. The Sooners fought their way back up to No. 3 in the rankings. That earned them the right to play top-ranked Penn State in the Orange Bowl. Bosworth and the rest of the defense held Penn State to just one touchdown in a 25–10 win. The Sooners had done enough to regain the No. 1 ranking in the final AP Poll. They were champions for the sixth time in school history.

Oklahoma had talented teams in 1986 and 1987. Each year they came into the season ranked first in the AP Poll. Just like in 1985, they lost one game each season. Both times it was again to Miami. The Hurricanes handed the Sooners their only loss three seasons in a row. Switzer stuck around for one more year. But the next 10 seasons would be among the hardest in team history.

CHAPTER 5

ONWARD, OKLAHOMA

Barry Switzer resigned in 1989 in the wake of recruiting violations. The NCAA put Oklahoma on probation for three years. The Sooners were not allowed to play on television in 1989. They could not play in bowl games in 1989 or 1990. And other limits were put on how much time coaches could spend with recruits.

The punishments kept Oklahoma from signing the top-flight athletes the program was accustomed to landing. That lack of quality recruits showed on the field. From 1989 to 1998, the team finished ranked in the AP Poll only three times. But then Bob Stoops arrived in 1999 from Florida. In just his second year, he helped lead the Sooners to their seventh national championship.

One of the main reasons behind the quick turnaround was the team's commitment to defense. From 2000 to 2003, the Sooners were among the nation's top six teams in points allowed.

Oklahoma linebacker Rocky Calmus makes a tackle against Air Force in 2001.

ROCKY CALMUS

Linebacker Rocky Calmus led the Sooners in tackles during his sophomore, junior, and senior years. He was an All-American as a junior and as a senior, and in 2001 he also won the Butkus Award. It is given each year to the best linebacker in the country. But perhaps the most impressive thing about Calmus was his toughness. He played most of the 2000 season with a broken bone near his thumb.

Stoops had worked as a defensive coordinator for 10 years at Kansas State and Florida before coming to Oklahoma. He coached some of the best defensive players in Oklahoma's history during those years. Linebackers Rocky Calmus and Teddy Lehman and defensive tackle Tommie Harris were each All-Americans twice during that four-season stretch.

That defense helped keep the Sooners near the top of the AP Poll in the four seasons after the 2000 national championship. But each year, the team came up just short of winning it all. In 2003 the Sooners had a powerful offense to match their tough defense. Junior quarterback Jason White broke the school record for touchdown passes in a season with 40. He also became Oklahoma's fourth Heisman Trophy winner.

The Sooners won their first 12 games of the season. But with the national championship on the line, Oklahoma again stumbled. Louisiana State (LSU) limited the Sooners to 154 yards of offense in a 21–14 loss in the Sugar Bowl.

White had another outstanding year in 2004. He threw for 3,205 yards and 35 touchdowns. Joining him in the backfield was

× Sooners quarterback Jason White won the 2003 Heisman Trophy and led the team to an undefeated regular season.

standout freshman running back Adrian Peterson. The All-American ran for 1,925 yards and 15 touchdowns. It was one of the best freshman college football seasons ever. Peterson finished second in Heisman Trophy voting, while White finished third.

Oklahoma running back Adrian Peterson runs for a touchdown during a 2005 game against Oklahoma State.

White and Peterson led the Sooners to another undefeated regular season in 2004. This time they won the Big 12 championship, crushing Colorado 42–3 in the conference title game. The Orange Bowl served as the national title game that year. But the game was not close. Oklahoma could not stop quarterback Matt Leinart of Southern California (USC), who had won the Heisman Trophy that year. Leinart threw for five touchdowns to crush Oklahoma's title dreams in a 55–19 loss.

Stoops had taken Oklahoma to the national championship game three times in his first six seasons as coach. And it would not be long before he had the Sooners back there. In 2007, three years after White graduated, another talented quarterback took over the team. Freshman Sam Bradford led an offense that scored more than 42 points per game. He threw for 3,121 yards and 36 touchdowns.

Bradford destroyed White's records the next season. In fact, Bradford had what might have been the best season by a quarterback in Sooners' history. In 2008 he threw for 4,720 yards and 50 touchdowns. He also won that year's Heisman Trophy. Along with Bradford, All-America tight end Jermaine Gresham and running backs Demarco Murray and Chris Brown helped the Sooners score just more than 51 points per game. That was the most in the country. The Sooners made the national championship game for the fourth time in Stoops's career as coach. But once again, the Sooners could not make the final push to get back to the top. Oklahoma lost 24–14 to Florida.

RECORD-SMASHING SAM

In just two seasons, Sam Bradford accomplished what it took previous Heisman Trophy winner Jason White a whole college career to do. Bradford's 50 touchdowns in 2008 were 10 more than White's single-season record from just five years earlier. And Bradford's 86 touchdown passes over his first two seasons broke White's Oklahoma career touchdown record of 81. Bradford returned for his junior year, but he was injured early in the season. He finished his Oklahoma career with 88 touchdown passes. The St. Louis Rams selected him first in the 2010 NFL Draft.

Baker Mayfield put up huge numbers as Oklahoma's quarterback from 2015 to 2017.

Bradford left for the NFL Draft after the 2009 season. Still, the Sooners remained one of the top teams in the country. Behind sophomore quarterback Landry Jones, Oklahoma won 12 games in 2010. That included a 48–20 win over Connecticut in the Fiesta Bowl.

Oklahoma's next on-field hero was an unlikely one. Quarterback Baker Mayfield received few scholarship offers after high school. He enrolled at Texas Tech as a walk-on in 2013. After a year, he transferred to Oklahoma. By 2015 he was the Sooners' starter. And he took them on a wild ride.

Mayfield threw for 3,700 yards and 37 touchdowns as the Sooners went 11–1 in 2015. They won the Big 12 and made their first appearance in the new College Football Playoff (CFP). In the national semifinals at the Orange Bowl, Oklahoma led Clemson 17–16 at the half, but the Tigers scored 21 unanswered points in the second to end the Sooners' season.

Mayfield was even better in 2016. He threw for 3,965 yards and 40 touchdowns. The Sooners stumbled down the stretch and missed the CFP, but they did beat Auburn in the Sugar Bowl.

That game was the last for Stoops. He announced his retirement from coaching the following summer. Stoops's 190 wins were the most in Oklahoma history, and his teams never had a losing record.

Replacing Stoops was a tough task. It fell to 33-year-old Oklahoma offensive coordinator Lincoln Riley. He became the youngest head coach in the top division of college football. Helping ease the transition was that he still had Mayfield at quarterback.

And Mayfield saved his best for last. In his final season he threw for 4,340 yards and 41 touchdowns and won the Heisman Trophy. The Sooners returned to the playoff and faced Georgia in the semifinals at the Rose Bowl. It was a thrilling, back-and-forth game. Oklahoma led 31–17 at half. Georgia stormed back to take a 38–31 lead. Mayfield tied it up again with a touchdown pass, and a defensive touchdown gave the Sooners a 45–38 lead with just under 7 minutes to play. But Georgia scored again in the final minute to force overtime.

After the teams traded field goals in the first overtime, the Sooners missed a short field goal in the second overtime. Two plays later, Georgia scored a touchdown to claim a 54–48 victory. It was a heartbreaking defeat for Oklahoma. And after the season, Mayfield was gone to the NFL.

Fortunately, the team had another elite quarterback waiting in the wings. Kyler Murray had to wait his turn behind Mayfield. But he made the most of his chance. The speedster threw for 4,054 yards and 40 touchdowns while running for 892 yards and 11 touchdowns in 2018. He was a true dual-threat quarterback and became the fourth Oklahoma signal-caller in the previous 15 years to win the Heisman Trophy.

Oklahoma again qualified for the CFP, but Murray and the Sooners were no match for Alabama. The Tide were up 21–0 before Murray even completed a pass. After just one amazing year as the Sooners' starter, Murray too left for the NFL.

Alabama got the win, but Oklahoma got their quarterback. Jalen Hurts transferred from the Tide to the Sooners before the 2019 season. Hurts had been a standout freshman at Alabama but lost his starting job. He instantly became the Sooners' starter and was another great dual threat like Murray. Hurts rushed for 1,298 yards and 20 touchdowns. He also passed for 3,851 yards and 32 touchdowns as his NFL Draft stock soared.

Hurts led the Sooners to another Big 12 championship and a spot in the CFP. But in the semifinals at the Peach Bowl, the Sooners ran

✕ Jalen Hurts had a huge impact in 2019, his only season with the Sooners.

into a buzz saw. Eventual national champion LSU rang up 49 points before halftime and routed Oklahoma 63–28. It was a tough way to end the season, but with four CFP appearances in five years, Sooners fans had to believe their next national championship was just around the corner.

TIMELINE

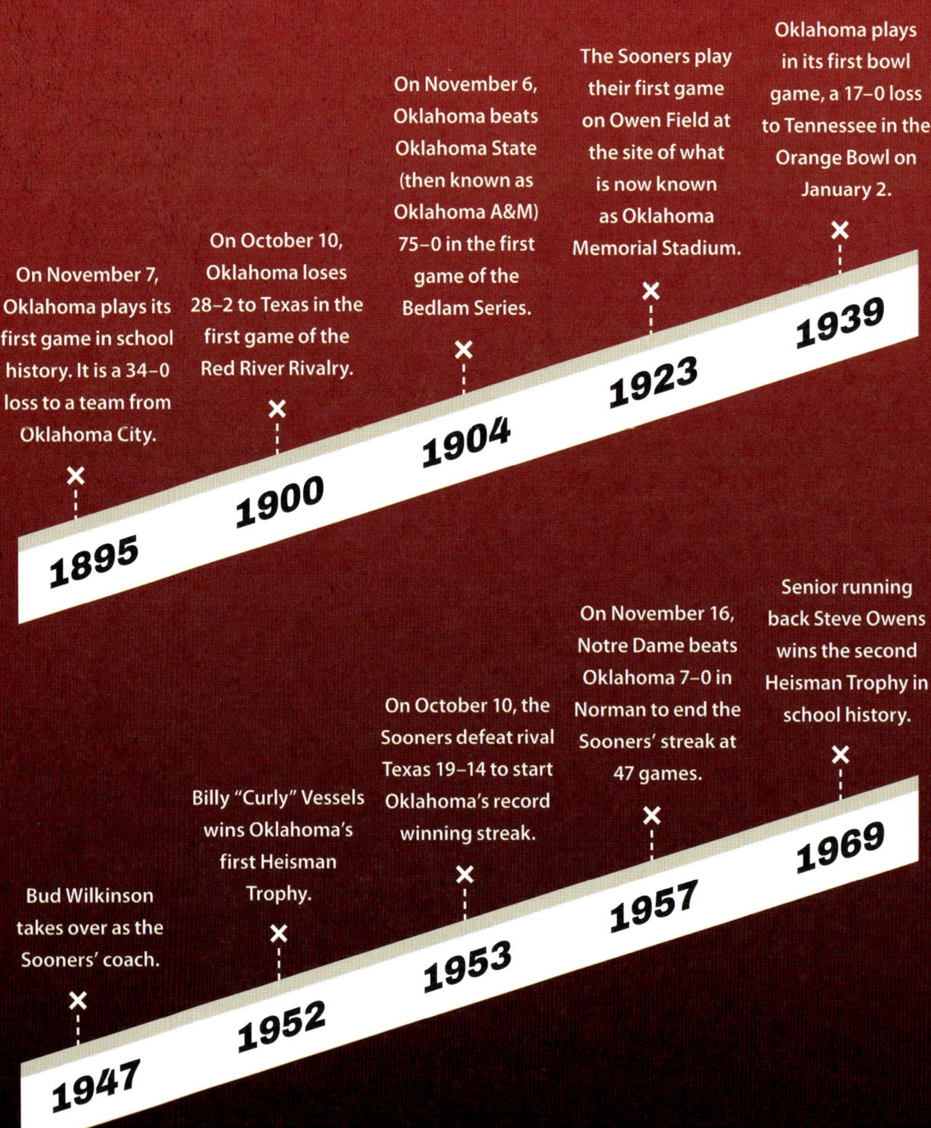

1895
On November 7, Oklahoma plays its first game in school history. It is a 34–0 loss to a team from Oklahoma City.
1900
On October 10, Oklahoma loses 28–2 to Texas in the first game of the Red River Rivalry.
1904
On November 6, Oklahoma beats Oklahoma State (then known as Oklahoma A&M) 75–0 in the first game of the Bedlam Series.
1923
The Sooners play their first game on Owen Field at the site of what is now known as Oklahoma Memorial Stadium.
1939
Oklahoma plays in its first bowl game, a 17–0 loss to Tennessee in the Orange Bowl on January 2.
1947
Bud Wilkinson takes over as the Sooners' coach.
1952
Billy "Curly" Vessels wins Oklahoma's first Heisman Trophy.
1953
On October 10, the Sooners defeat rival Texas 19–14 to start Oklahoma's record winning streak.
1957
On November 16, Notre Dame beats Oklahoma 7–0 in Norman to end the Sooners' streak at 47 games.
1969
Senior running back Steve Owens wins the second Heisman Trophy in school history.

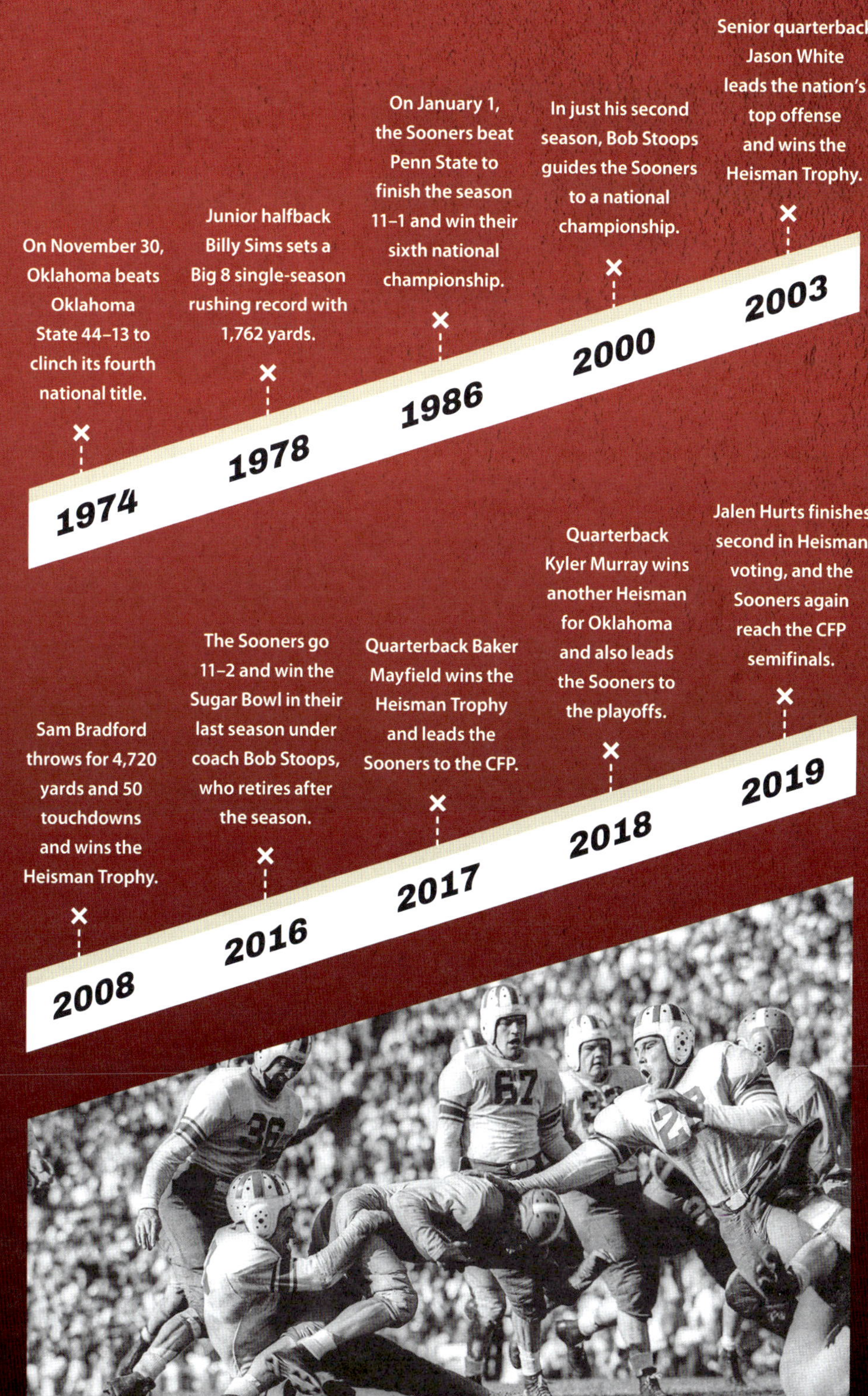

1974 — On November 30, Oklahoma beats Oklahoma State 44–13 to clinch its fourth national title.

1978 — Junior halfback Billy Sims sets a Big 8 single-season rushing record with 1,762 yards.

1986 — On January 1, the Sooners beat Penn State to finish the season 11–1 and win their sixth national championship.

2000 — In just his second season, Bob Stoops guides the Sooners to a national championship.

2003 — Senior quarterback Jason White leads the nation's top offense and wins the Heisman Trophy.

2008 — Sam Bradford throws for 4,720 yards and 50 touchdowns and wins the Heisman Trophy.

2016 — The Sooners go 11–2 and win the Sugar Bowl in their last season under coach Bob Stoops, who retires after the season.

2017 — Quarterback Baker Mayfield wins the Heisman Trophy and leads the Sooners to the CFP.

2018 — Quarterback Kyler Murray wins another Heisman for Oklahoma and also leads the Sooners to the playoffs.

2019 — Jalen Hurts finishes second in Heisman voting, and the Sooners again reach the CFP semifinals.

QUICK STATS

PROGRAM INFO

University of Oklahoma Rough Riders, Boomers (1898–1908)
University of Oklahoma Sooners (1908–)

NATIONAL CHAMPIONSHIPS

1950, 1955, 1956, 1974*, 1975, 1985, 2000

OTHER ACHIEVEMENTS

Conference titles: 48
CFP appearances: 2015, 2017, 2018, 2019
Bowl record: 29–23–1

KEY COACHES

Lincoln Riley (2017–)
36–6, 0–3 (bowl games)
Bob Stoops (1999–2016)
190–48, 9–9 (bowl games)
Barry Switzer (1973–88)
157–29–4, 8–5 (bowl games)
Bud Wilkinson (1947–63)
145–29–4, 6–2 (bowl games)

KEY PLAYERS

Brian Bosworth (LB, 1983–86)
Sam Bradford (QB, 2007–09)**
Rocky Calmus (LB, 1998–2001)
Josh Heupel (QB, 1999–2000)
Jalen Hurts (QB, 2019)
Keith Jackson (TE, 1984–87)
Baker Mayfield (QB, 2015–17)**
Tommy McDonald (HB, 1954–56)
Kyler Murray (QB, 2018)**
Steve Owens (RB, 1967–69)**
Adrian Peterson (RB, 2004–06)
Lee Roy Selmon (DT, 1972–75)
Billy Sims (HB, 1975–79)**
Billy Vessels (HB, 1950–52)**
Jason White (QB, 1999–2004)**

HOME STADIUM

Gaylord Family–Oklahoma Memorial Stadium (1923–)

*Denotes shared title
**Heisman Trophy winner
All statistics through 2019 season

QUOTES & ANECDOTES

Bud Wilkinson stayed busy after he left the sidelines at Oklahoma. He retired from coaching to run for the US Senate, but that was unsuccessful. Then he became a sports analyst on ABC television from 1965 to 1977. Wilkinson, who had a master's degree in English, also was a member of the White House staff from 1969 to 1971. But he just could not keep himself away from football. He returned to the game for two years, in 1978 and 1979, when he coached the NFL's St. Louis Cardinals.

Brian Bosworth was one of the best linebackers to ever play college football. He was also one of the most controversial. He was known for his crazy hairstyles and for sharing his opinions about everything, no matter who might be offended. Before the 1987 Orange Bowl, Bosworth was suspended for using steroids. Then on the sidelines at the game, he wore a shirt that criticized the NCAA. Oklahoma coach Barry Switzer decided to kick him off the team.

"Whatever is said before, during, or after has no effect on the game. It's what happens during the 60 minutes of the game, out there on the floor of the Cotton Bowl that counts. This is no ordinary game, as anyone who has ever played or seen it would tell you."

—Oklahoma Sooners coach Barry Switzer on the Red River Rivalry with Texas. The Oklahoma-Texas game was held in the Cotton Bowl stadium for many years.

GLOSSARY

All-America
Designation for players chosen as the best amateurs in the country in a particular sport.

athletic director
An administrator who oversees the coaches, players, and teams of an institution.

conference
A group of schools that join together to create a league for their sports teams.

coordinator
An assistant coach who is in charge of the offense or defense.

draft
A system that allows teams to acquire new players coming into a league.

favored
Expected to win.

momentum
The strength or force that allows something to continue or to grow stronger.

probation
A period of time when a person or team is punished for wrongdoing.

recruiting
Convincing a high school player to attend a certain college, usually to play sports.

retired
Ended one's career.

rivalry
A fierce and ongoing competition between two players or teams.

upset
An unexpected victory by a supposedly weaker team.

MORE INFORMATION

BOOKS

Campbell, Dave. *The Story of the Orange Bowl*. Minneapolis, MN: Abdo Publishing, 2016.

Wilner, Barry. *The Story of the College Football National Championship Game*. Minneapolis, MN: Abdo Publishing, 2016.

York, Andy. *Ultimate College Football Road Trip*. Minneapolis, MN: Abdo Publishing, 2019.

ONLINE RESOURCES

To learn more about the Oklahoma Sooners, please visit **abdobooklinks.com** or scan this QR code. These links are routinely monitored and updated to provide the most current information available.

PLACES TO VISIT

College Football Hall of Fame
cfbhall.com

This hall of fame and museum in Atlanta, Georgia, highlights the greatest players and moments in the history of college football. Among the former Sooners enshrined here are Billy Vessels, Steve Owens, Keith Jackson, Lee Roy Selmon, and Joe Washington.

Gaylord Family–Oklahoma Memorial Stadium
soonersports.com/sports/2019/8/12/208803887

This has been Oklahoma's home field since 1923. It was named in honor of Oklahomans who died in World War I. After several major renovations, the stadium holds 80,126 spectators.

INDEX

ABOUT THE AUTHOR

Todd Ryan is a library assistant from the Upper Peninsula of Michigan. He lives near Houghton with his two cats, Izzo and Mooch.